A selection of words and anecdotes
from around Suffolk

by
Louise Maskill

BRADWELL
BOOKS

1

Published by Bradwell Books
9 Orgreave Close Sheffield S13 9NP
Email: books@bradwellbooks.co.uk

© Louise Maskill 2014

British Library Cataloguing in Publication Data:
a catalogue record for this book is available from the
British Library.

1st Edition

ISBN: 9781902674889

Print: Gomer Press, Llandysul, Ceredigion SA44 4JL

Artwork and design by: Andrew Caffrey

SUFFOLK DIALECT

by Louise Maskill

ACKNOWLEDGEMENTS

This book came together at the request and with the support of Chris Gilbert; I am indebted to him for research materials, guidance and for his continued faith in me. Tom, Molly, Owen and Caitlin have encouraged me throughout and made their own contributions to the A-to-Z, and have also provided a good deal of moral support. Tom also found errors aplenty in early drafts; any that remain in the book are my responsibility, not his.

Huge thanks to all of you.

DEDICATION

For Molly, Owen and Caitlin

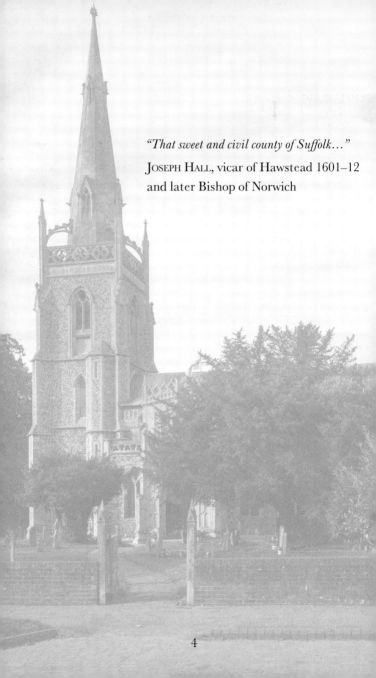

"That sweet and civil county of Suffolk…"
JOSEPH HALL, vicar of Hawstead 1601–12
and later Bishop of Norwich

Introduction

Although dialects are still evident in everyday speech from different parts of the country, they are nowhere near as common or as diverse as they used to be. This gradual extinction has been noted and mourned by writers and antiquarians over many years, and huge efforts have been made to capture the colloquial speech of men and women from various parts of the country.

The Icenian dialects of the eastern counties (as they were described by Robert Forby in his 1830 book on The Vocabulary of East Anglia) are rich and vivid, but the Norfolk and Suffolk dialects are often lumped together in popular consciousness (along with Somerset) into a kind of generic rural vernacular. They are clearly similar, but there are distinct and significant differences between them; my childhood in Norfolk meant I was familiar with a lot of the terms you will find in this book, but there are many that are new to me, or which are used in different ways.

The first part of this book is an A to Z of words and phrases arranged with their meanings and a few examples of usage, while the second part contains a collection of anecdotes, stories, rhymes and curiosities, all arranged by theme. Some of the words in the A to Z are now in common use in everyday English, but the aim is to indicate their provenance in the old Suffolk dialect. The anecdotes may be long or short, complicated or simple, but all contain genuine examples of Suffolk dialect as gathered by myself or recorded by historians and collectors over the years.

Louise Maskill

Leiston village post office, 1908.

A

Aatanune – afternoon

Abroad – a long way off, in distant parts

About – near to, nearly

"Is the horse worth forty pounds?" "Naw, nothing about it."

Adays – shortened version of nowadays

Addle or aidle – to grow or thrive (as in a crop), or to earn or save up gradually

It took me years ter addle up the money.

Afeared – frightened, afraid

Again – against, or near to

Agreeable – compliant, in agreement with a proposal

Ague (pron. agah) – a cold or inflammation

Ahuh – aslant, askew or awry

Allost or ollus – always

Allus, ellus or ullus – ale house

Anberry – a small swelling or pustule on a horse, or a small knob on a turnip or other root vegetable

Apple-jack – a pudding made by folding sliced apples and sugar inside pastry and baking

Aren't – am not

Argufy – to have impact, to signify

What does that argufy?

Arsle – to move backwards, or to fidget

Arselins – backwards

Arsy-farsy – vice versa, back to front

Ashup, eshup or ushup – ash heap

Atter – pus. Hence *attery*, rotten or gangrenous

Avised – aware of, informed about

Are you avised of that?

B

Bab – to fish using a single worm-baited line weighted with lead. Commonly used to catch eels inland, or crabs on the coast

Badget – a badger

Badly – in poor health

Balder – to use coarse language. Hence the original meaning of balderdash – filthy or obscene talk

Bamble – to walk unsteadily and weakly

Ban – to curse

How she did ban and blast!

Bandy – a hare, from the shape of its back legs

Bang – a particular type of hard dry cheese made from milk skimmed several times. Also known as *Suffolk thump*

Bargain – a lot; an indefinite quantity

Barley-bird – a rural name for the nightingale (because it arrives during barley-sowing season)

Basking – a drenching in a heavy shower

Bavish – to drive away or banish

Being – an abode or habitation

Betty boil – a tea kettle

Bibble – to eat like a duck, taking food and drink into the mouth together

Bishop-barnabee (or bishy barnabee) – a common East Anglian term for the ladybird

Blee – resemblance, look

That boy has a strong blee of his father.

Blood-fallen – chilblained

Blore – to bellow like a bull

Bobbish – pretty good, quite clever

Bor, borh – boy, a term of familiar address. Applied to all ages and sexes, although it was common for elderly folk to address their juniors as *bor*

Bottle-bump – the bittern

Bravely – very much recovered after sickness

Brig – a bridge

Broad – a lake formed by the expansion of a river in flat country

Broak or brock – to belch

Buffle-headed – foolish or confused

Bull-feist – the common puffball fungus

Burr – a mistiness over or around the moon

Busk – of fowls or chickens, to take a dust bath on a hot dry day

Butter-teeth – an individual with broad and yellowed teeth

Button – a small cake

Bures village, the Queen's Head Inn, 1904

C

Caddow – a jackdaw

Cail – to throw weakly and inaccurately, or to move with a meandering and irregular gait

Call – to hurl abusive names

Callow – the layer of earth above a layer of gravel, sand etc., which must be removed to reach it (in a process of *uncallowing*)

Calmy – motherly, nurturing

Camp – an ancient, athletic and violent team ballgame, a forerunner of football, once played across East Anglia

Camping land or camping ground – a piece of land set aside for the game of camp

Canker-rose – the common red field poppy (also known as the *copper rose* or *headache*)

Cant – to throw something upwards suddenly or abruptly

Caps – fungi

Casualty – any animal that has died by chance, rather than from disease or at the slaughterhouse

Catch-rogue – a bailiff, sheriff or constable; anyone whose job it is to apprehend offenders

Caunsey – a raised or paved road; a causeway

Chads – dry husky fragments found in food. Inferior quality bread may be said to be *chaddy*

Chamble – to chew food finely and thoroughly

Chatterpie – a magpie

Check – to taunt or reproach

Chick – a flaw or chip in pottery or earthenware

Chill – to take extreme coldness off a beverage, often by placing it near a fire or heat source. The opposite of modern usage

Chingle – gravel, small stones

Chink – a sprain in the back

Chop-logger-head – a blockhead or idiot, who has a head thick enough to chop logs on

Chout – a rustic frolic or merry-making

Chubby – surly or grumpy

Chuffy – fat and fleshy, especially about the face
and cheeks

Chump – a thick log of wood

Claggy – clogged with moisture. Especially applied to
mud on footpaths

Clart – to daub with syrup, honey, jam etc. Hence *clarty* –
sticky, syrupy

Clever – neat, elegant; or dextrous, adroit,
good with the hands

Clim – an imp that inhabits the chimneys of nurseries

Climp – to touch a shiny surface with greasy fingers
and leave marks behind

Clip – to shear sheep, or the wool resulting from
sheep shearing

   Farmer Smith had but a moderate clip this year.

Clod-hopper – a farmer or agricultural labourer

Clough – a ravine with steep banks and a run of water at
the bottom

Coarse – applied to weather; the opposite of fine

   Tis a coarse sort of morning.

Cob – a seagull

Come-back – a guinea-fowl (from its distinctive call)

Company-keeper – a lover

Condition – temper, disposition

Cope – a large quantity or a great number

Coxy-roxy – merrily and enthusiastically tipsy

Crag – a deposit of fossil seashells, commonly used as a soil improver on farmland

Crawly-mawly – weakly and ailing

Crickle or chuckle – to sink or bend under excessive weight

Crimble – to creep or sneak about

Crome – a staff with a hook at the end, used for pulling down tree branches, rescuing small boys from ditches and so on

Croodle – to lie snugly and tucked up warm with bedfellows, as puppies or piglets do

Crow-keeper – a boy employed to scare crows from new-sown land

Crow-time – evening, when the crows fly back to their roosts

Crumplin – a small or malformed apple, or (possibly by extension) a small person

Culp – a hard and heavy blow

Curous – curious

Cute – sharp, quick to apprehend and understand

D

Dabby – moist and apt to cling to the flesh, like wet linen

Daddle – walk unsteadily, like a small child

Dag – dew, or early morning or evening mist

Dag of rain – a slight and misty shower

Dangerous – endangered

Mr North is quite sadly badly; very dangerous.

Daunt – to stun or knock down

Deal-tree – the fir tree

Dee – a dice

Dere – dire, dreadful. Hence *derely* – dreadfully, lamentably

Develin – the swift, so-named for its black plumage and devilish screeching

Dicky – an ass or donkey

Ding – to throw with a quick motion; or to beat or hit repeatedly

I dung it at him.

Dint, dent or dant – didn't

Doated – decayed or rotten, as of old trees

Doddy or doody – a short person

Dodman or hodman – a snail

Dome or doom – down or fluff from a young animal such as a rabbit, a chicken etc.

Dor – a cockchafer

Doss – to attack with horns, as of a ram, bull or goat

Dowler – a coarse dumpling

Downfall – a descent from the clouds. Rain, hail, snow

Drant – to drone or drawl when speaking

Drepe – to drip or dribble

Driv – drove

Duddle – to cover closely and snugly with blankets

Dunt – stupid or dizzy-headed

Dut – do it

Duzzy or dauzy – confused or confusing

Dwain, dwainy – sickly or faint

Dwile – a waste lock of wool, or a mop made from such fibres used for mopping dishes

E

Eachon – each one

Ebble – the aspen tree

Eddish – the aftermath

Eldern – the elder tree

Elvish – peevish or wantonly mischievous

The bees are very elvish today.

Erriwiggle – an earwig

Even-flavoured – uniform, unvarying

It was an even-flavoured day of rain.

Ewe – owed

He ewe me a fiver.

Hintlesham village, 1906

F

Fagot – a contemptuous name for lazy or useless woman

Fall – to let fall or bring down

I shall fall that tree come spring.

Fang – a fin

Fangast – a marriageable girl

Fapes or japes – gooseberries

Fare – to seem

She fared quite sickly.

Farmer – the eldest son of the owner/occupier of a farm
(see master below)

Feft – to persuade, or try to persuade

Fen nightingale – a frog. Also known as a *march bird*

Filands – fields, unenclosed arable land

Fit – ready

Come, stir, get yourself fit!

Fizmer – to fidget or make a great deal of fuss about a trifling matter

Flacky – to hang loose

Flap – a slight touch or stroke of illness

I have but a flap of cold.

Flaps – large broad mushrooms

Flarnecking – flaunting, in a vulgar and ostentatious manner

Fleet – shallow, as of a dish or basin, or else a ditch or pond

Flush – the stream from a mill-wheel

Fogger – a street seller or pedlar, often travelling between villages on a seasonal round

Foky – bloated, soft

Forced – to be obliged, unable to avoid doing something

I was forced to go.

Forgive – to start to thaw

Frail – to pick at or wear our cloth

Freeli-frailies – light insubstantial snacks or delicacies for the high tea table

Frenchman – any man of any country who can't speak English

Fresh – tipsy

Fresher – a small frog

Frightful – apt to take fright

Frowy – stale, or on the point of turning sour. Usually applied to dairy products

Frump – a sour ill-tempered person, especially applied to old women

Fuzzy – rough or shaggy

Snape village sugar beet for Holland 1909

G

Gag – to reject with loathing, or to nauseate

Gain – handy, dextrous; or desirable, good, just as it should be
  I bought this horse very gain.

Gallont – a gallon

18

Gander – to gad or gamble about

Gang – a number of the same sort of thing, all together. Commonly applied to people, but may also be used for inanimate objects such as boats or ploughs

Ganger – a fast horse, a goer

Ganty-gutted – gaunt, lean and lanky

Gartless – heedless, thoughtless

Gay-cards – the picture cards in a pack

Ge – to go

Gear – stuff, tackle, equipment of any sort. May be applied to professions, e.g. a doctor's gear

Giffle – to be restless or fidgety

Gim, gimmy – neat and smart

Gimble – to make a face, grin or smile

Glent or glint – a glimpse, a short fleeting view

Glusky – sulky

Goaf – a rick of corn or straw laid up in a barn

Goaf-flap – a wooden beater to knock the ends of goafs level. Seldom used in Suffolk, but often employed in practical jokes

Go-by-the-ground – a derogatory term for a short person

Gobbler – a turkey-cock

Golls – fat cheeks or jowls, or folds of fat on the body of a corpulent person

Good-doing – charitable, fond of good works

The parson's daughters are very good-doing young women.

Goose-gog – a gooseberry

Gore – mud, mire

Goslin – the male willow catkin, from the fact that it is soft and yellow and resembles a newly hatched goose

Grass-widow – a young girl whose 'nuptials' were not celebrated in church but on the grass, and whose beloved has deserted her

Grease – a faint covering of clouds in the sky

The sky's greasing up; we shall soon have rain.

Green-olp – a greenfinch

Grewin – a greyhound

Grigs – small eels

Grimble – to begrime, smudge or cover with dirt

Grimmer – a wide pond or mere covered in weeds

Grindle – a small and narrow drain for water

Grissens – stairs

Groaning – a lying-in, a birthing

Groaning cake – a cake made to accompany a groaning (perhaps to keep the attendants sustained)

Ground-rain – a plentiful, constant but light fall of rain, which works its way deep into the ground

Grub – idle and nonsensical talk

Grub-felling – felling trees by undermining them and cutting their roots

Grunny – the snout of a hog

Gull – to sweep away by force of running water

The bank has been gulled away by the flood.

Gush – a gust of wind

Gussock – a strong and sudden gust of wind

H

Hackle – to tether beasts to prevent escape

Haggy – broken or uneven and wet soil. If the soil dries out it becomes *hobbley*

Hake – to toil or work with great effort and labour

Half-rocked – oafish or silly

Hand-smooth – uninterrupted, without obstacle or imperfection

Hang – a crop of fruit

Hang-nail – a raised and hardened potion of the cuticle sticking up at the base or side of a fingernail

Harder – the hornbeam tree, commonly used in hedging

Harnsey or harnser – a heron

Harnsey-gutted – lanky and lean, like a heron

Harriage – to be all in confusion

They're all of a harriage.

Hassock – a tussock of grass, especially in a mire or bog

Hassock-head – a person sporting a bushy growth of hair

Hawkey or horky – the feast of harvest home

Hawkey-load – the last load of the harvest, brought home with great ceremony

Hay – a hedge

Hay-jack – a variety of sparrow

Haze – to dry linen by hanging it on a hedge in the sun

Head – the face

I told him so to his head.

Headswoman – a midwife

Heads and holls – pell mell, confusion

Heir – to inherit

His son will heir the estate.

Hen's nose-full – a minute quantity

Het – have it

Himp – to limp

Hire – to borrow

Hitch – to move along or shift slightly something that happens to be in the way

Hitch your chair along to make room.

Hitty-missy – hit or miss, at random

Hobbles – lumps or roughness in a road or path

Hobby-lantern – a will o' the wisp

Hoddy – well in health and spirits

Hoist – a cough

Holl – a dry ditch

Hooly or hully – very, fairly

Hop-crease -- the game of hopscotch

Hornpie – the lapwing

Hudderin – a well-grown lad

> *"How many men do you have on the farm?"*
> *"Two men and a hudderin."*

Huff – a dry, scurfy or scaly skin condition

Hull – to throw

Hullup – to vomit

Hulver – holly

Hunch – a lift or shove, such as might be given to a fat person trying to mount a horse

Hunch-weather – cold weather that makes one hunch one's shoulders

Hunger-poisoned – famished, unhealthy through lack of food. Commonly applied to misers

Flempton village smithy, 1906

I

Ichon – each one, every one

Ill-conditioned – bad-tempered

Imitate – to try or attempt something

A toddler might *imitate to walk*

Indifferent – ill, poorly

Innocent – silly or naïve

Innards, inwards – intestines

J

Jacob – a toad

Jade – a horse

Jag – an indefinite quantity of something

Jammock – to beat, squash or pummel into a pulp

Jasper – a wasp

Jibby – a saucy young girl

Jilly-hooter – an owl

Jim – a type of two-wheeled cart or vehicle

Jink – to sprain or twist a joint

Jossing block – a mounting block

Jot – downright, straight

He fell down jot on his backside.

K

Kedge, kedgy – brisk, active

Kett – carrion

Kicky – showy

Kindiful – kindly, well-meaning

Kinked – entangled, knotted, as in thread or yarn

Kinsman – relational term applied specifically to nephews

Kisky – dry, husky

Kittle – to tickle

Kitty-witch – a type of crab with fringed claws, common along the east coast

Knock – to walk or bowl briskly along

He come knocking along in a great hurry.

Know – knowledge

Know-nothing – poor fool, ignorant person

L

Lace – to thrash or beat

Ladle – dawdle

Lagarag – a lazy fellow

Lall – to lounge or loiter (as a lagarag might)

Lap – thin broth or porridge, or weak tea

Lash, lashy – applied to fruit, soft and watery

Lay – a very large pond, or a coarse old pasture

Learn or larn – to teach

Leasty – applied to weather, dull and wet

Ledge – a bar on a gate or on a chair or table

Lick-up – a pittance or miserably small amount, particularly of food or drink

Link – a sausage, or a string of them

Listly – quick of hearing

Lob – to kick

Lobster or mousehunt – a stoat

Loke – a short narrow dead-end lane

Loose-ended – vulgar, crude

   She was a loose-ended baggage.

Lorker – a seagull

Lugsome – heavy, cumbersome

Lumber – coarse or foolish talk

Lump – to hit or beat with heavy blows

M

Macaroon – a fop or dandy

Mag – to chatter

Magotty – whimsical, freakish

Mamble – to eat without relish or with disinterest

Mammocks – leavings, wasted fragments

March-bird – a frog

Mardle – to gossip, pass the time of day; or a pond near a house, in a yard or on a village green, convenient for watering cattle

Master – used to refer to the owner/occupier of a farm

Matchly – exactly alike, fitting well together

Mavis – a thrush

Maukin – a scarecrow

Mauther or mawther – a young girl

Meaning – a hint or a likelihood

I have a meaning of a fever this morning.

Measled – diseased

Mim – primly silent

Ming – to knead, as of bread dough

Minnock – someone who affects delicacy and refined airs

Miscasualty – an unlucky accident

Misery – pain in any part of the body

Mislon-bush – mistletoe

Moil – to labour, work hard

Moise – to improve or increase

Molt – profuse perspiration. Hence *molted* – badly affected by heat

Mort – a very great quantity

Mozy – shaggy, covered in hair

Muckup – muck heap

Muck-grubber – a sordid and scrounging saver of money

Muddled – worn out, exhausted

Mug – gloomy damp weather, or light rain

Mulder – to crumble into dust

Mulligrubs or mulps – a fit of the sulks.
Hence *mulpy*, sulky

Mumper – a beggar or tramp

Mure-hearted – soft-hearted, meek spirited, easily
moved to pity or tears

Aldeburgh Beach Huts 1899

N

Nabbity – short in stature, although full-grown.
Sometimes applied to a short woman

Nabble – to gnaw or nibble

Nab-nanny – a louse in the hair

Narrow-wriggle – an earwig

Native – hometown or birthplace

Ipswich is my native.

Nattle – to bustle and hustle about trifling matters

Naughty-back – a gentle form of reproach, usually applied to children

Nay-word – a password

Near – penny-pinching, miserly

Near-now – a little while ago

Nervish – nervous, affected by weakness of nerves

Nettlespring – nettle rash

Newdicle – something new-fangled and miraculous

News – to report or tell as news

It was newsed about at market this morning.

Niffle, niffle-naffle – to trifle, or play at one's work

Nip – to be parsimonious in domestic management

Noah's Ark – a cloud appearing in an otherwise clear sky, resembling a large boat hull-side up. A sure sign of rain

Noils – coarse refuse locks of wool

No matters – moderate, nothing to boast about

The squire is no matters of a shot.

Nonnock – a whim or childish fancy

Nor – than

Notchet – a notable feat, something which deserves to be recorded

Nowl, noble – the navel

Num – stupid

Nunty – plain, old-fashioned (when applied to female attire)

Nutcrome – a stick with a crook at the end, used to pull down boughs of nut trees for harvesting

O

Odious – ill-smelling or ill-tasting

Old – customary or usual

Old Shock or Old Shuck – a spirit in the shape of a great black dog (or sometimes a calf) which haunts highways and footpaths in the dark

Old sows – woodlice

Olland – arable land which has been laid to pasture for two years or longer

Ont or wont – will not

Opinion – to give one's thoughts

I opinion so.

Ought – nought, zero

Over-flush – an excess or superfluity of something

Over-give – to thaw or melt

Overwhart – across or at right-angles to something else

Owe – to possess by right

Mr Jones owes that farm.

P

Pack-gate – a gate on a pack-way, once commonly used by pack-horses

Pad – to make a path by walking on an untrodden surface, as over newly-ploughed land or fresh snow

Paigle – a cowslip

Pample – to trample lightly

Panchion – a large broad pan

Pash – to break or beat anything brittle into small fragments

Pass – to pass the bell is to ring a bell for the purposes of announcing a death

Patch-upon – to unjustly accuse or blame wrongfully
  He patched it upon me.

Paved – turned hard, like clay soil in dry weather

Ped – a pannier or basket with a lid

Pedder – one who carries wares to market in a *ped*, and sells from it when he gets there

Pend – to press or pinch, as in a shoe that is too tight

Pense, pensy – fretful, uneasy

Perk – a perch, or to perch on something

Perries – fairies. Hence *perry-dancers* – the northern lights (aurora borealis)

Peterman – a fisherman (by association with the apostle Peter)

Pickcheese – the titmouse or wren

Piclle – to glean or harvest a second time

Pie-wipe – the lapwing or peewit

Pightle, pitle or picle – a field or piece of enclosed land

Pike off! – begone! Go away!

Pingle – to pick at one's food

Pin-patches – periwinkles (because they are eaten from their shells with a pin)

Piss-bed – the common dandelion

Pit-hole – a grave

Planger – a boarded floor

Plaw – to parboil

Pluggy – thick-set and sturdy

Pod – a fat belly

Poke – a bag

Polt – a hard blow

Poppet or poppin – a puppy or a puppet

Popple – a poplar tree

Pose – a cold in the head

Pot-ladles – tadpoles (from their shape)

Power – a great number

There was a vast power of folks at market today.

Prest – soon, presently

I shall be with you prest.

Pritch – a strong sharp implement for making holes, e.g. for fence posts

Pulk – a hole full of mud, or a small muddy pond
Punch – short, stocky
Pur – a poker
Purdy – surly, ill-tempered, self-important
Purely – much improved in health after a spell of illness
I am purely today, thank you.

Monks Eleigh village, 1908

Q

Quackle – to choke
Quaddle or quoddle – to coddle or boil gently
Quaddy – very broad and short, especially applied
to a person

Quaggy – soft, wobbly, tremulous. Often applied to very wet mud, but may also be used to describe corpulent people

Quail – to curdle or go off

Quavery-mavery – undecided, hesitant

Quezzen – to suffocate with poisonous gas, or to smother. A damp fire is said to quezzen out

R

Rack – a rut in the road, e.g. a cart-rack

Raff – rubbish, worthless fragments

Raft – a musty damp smell. Hence *rafty, raftiness*

Rake – to ramble idly. Sometimes applied to truant children

Rally – a coarse sieve, used for sifting soil

Ramp – to prance or romp, or (of plants) to grow profusely and rapidly

Ramshackled – confused and obstructed in action or intention, like a ram who is shackled (his foreleg tied to his head collar)

Ranch – to scratch deeply with a nail or other pointed instrument

Rand – a joint of beef

Ranny – a shrew

Rase – to scratch or cut superficially

Rasp or resp – to belch

Rather of the ratherest – a very little too much. Sometimes applied to one who is half drunk

Rattock – a great noise

Red-weed – any type of poppy with red flowers

Ret – to soak in water

Retting pit – a pit for soaking

Rid – rode

Right – to set in order

Right up the room, company is coming.

Rip – to swear profusely in anger

Rising – yeast or other raising agent

Riz – risen

Roke – a fog

Rommock – to gambol or romp boisterously

Rove – a scab

Ruck – a wrinkle or crease

Rum – odd, strange, inexplicable

Ruttle – to make a harsh noise in the chest when breathing

S

Sad-bad, sadly-badly – very poorly, very ill

Sag – to collapse through weakness

Sally – a hare

Sanny – to whine or wail without apparent cause

Scald – a multitude or collection of something insignificant

Scantity – a scarcity or shortage

Scoot – an irregular projection of wall or fence marring the regular shape of a field, garden etc.

Scotch – to spare or refrain from doing something

I did not scotch to tell her my mind.

Scrab – scratch or claw

Scrabbled eggs – a dish commonly eaten during Lent, made of hard-boiled eggs with butter, salt and pepper

Scranch or scrange – a deep scratch

Scrimmage – a fight or skirmish. Still commonly applied to football and other team sports

Scrog-legs – bandy or crooked legs

Seal – a time or season of the farming year

See – saw

Selled – sold

Set – astonished, astounded

When she heard the news she was quite set.

Sew – sewn, sewed

Tom Smith he sew a furrow, but his wife she sew a seam.

Several – a useful word meaning anything from a few to a great many

Shack – to rove about or wander, as a tramp does. Also used to describe a shabby fellow or vagrant; hence *shacky*, shabby or ragged

Shant – shall not

Sheer – shining red with inflammation

Sheres – all other parts of the world apart from the sister counties of Suffolk and Norfolk (and sometimes Essex). Hence *shere-man*, a foreigner

Shew – showed

Shitten-Saturday – the Saturday in Passion Week, when Jesus' body lay enclosed in the tomb.
From Shut-In Saturday

Shive – a small thin slice

Sholt – a mangy dog, a cur

Shoring – aslant, askew or awry

Shove (pron. to rhyme with grove) – to lose milk teeth

Shug – to shake

Shunt – should not

Shutting in – evening, the time when doors, windows and curtains are closed

Sidlings, sidus – sideways

Silly-bold – impertinent or unseemly

Sin, sen – since

Skelp – to kick with violence

Skew – to start sideways, as a horse might

Skinch – to stint and give short measure

Skink – to serve drinks at table

Slar, slare – to bedaub or slather

Slatter – to wash carelessly or splash with water. Hence *slattering weather* – frequent light rain

Slent – a gentle slope in the ground

Slub – thick sticky mud

Slur – loose thin mud. The opposite of slub

Slush – light mud, or filthy talk. Hence *slushy* – foul-mouthed

Smeath – a large area of open ground

Smur – light misty rain

Snick or sneck – a latch or fastening on a door

Sneer – to pull faces, without the intention to insult

Snickle – a slip-knot

Snippock – a tiny morsel

Sort – a great number

Soss – a jumble or mixed mess of food

Spending-cheese – middling quality cheese kept by dairymen for family consumption after the inferior bang had been sold off to the Navy

Spink – a chaffinch

Spirit – a lightning strike

    A spirit lit upon the church steeple during the storm.

Spoffle – to be over-busy doing very little

Sprunny – neat, tidy, spruce

Spud – anything particularly short for its kind. Hence *spuddy* – very short and stumpy

Spuffle – to move along hastily and busily; to bustle

Squat – to quieten or silence. Hence *squatting pills* – sleeping tablets or painkillers

    Nurse, squat that child!

Squinder – to burn faintly, like damp fuel

Squinny – to squint

Squit – utter nonsense

Stanstickle – the stickleback fish

Stew – a cloud of dust, as from a busy road in the summer

Stilts – crutches

Stive – dust

Stover – winter food for cattle

Strip – to milk a cow to the point where the udders are empty

Stry – to waste or destroy wantonly. Hence *stryance* – wastefulness

Sucklin – honeysuckle, or the common purple clover

Suffen – something

Swailing – lurching from side to side while walking

Swash or swashy – swaggering, blustering

Swidge – a puddle or splash of water

Swottling – corpulent, greasy, sweaty

Emsett village, 1909

T

Ta, te, to – the

Tan – then, used often in now and tan

Tantrums – airs, whims, absurd ideas

Tea – used as a verb to describe the afternoon meal in the same sense as dine

My neighbour is to tea with me tomorrow.

Tebbin – it has been

Teen – trouble, vexation, annoyance

Terrify – to tease or annoy

Thack – to thatch a roof, or any material used for thatching

Them – those. Often *them-there*
  Whose are them-there books?

There and there-aways – thereabouts

Thought – a very minute difference in degree. Something may be a thought too wide, long, heavy etc.

Thrum – to purr, as a cat does

Thump – alternative name for Suffolk bang, the characteristic hard cheese sold to the Navy

Tick – a very gentle touch, by way of a non-verbal hint or token or encouragement or endearment

Tiddling, tittling – the topmost. Something may be the *tiddling top*

Tiff – a slight temper or anger

Tight – prompt, active, alert

Tip – a smart but light blow

Tipe – to overbalance and fall headlong because of being top-heavy

Together – commonly used to address a group of persons collectively
  Well, together, how are ye all?

Tolerate – to domineer or tyrannise

Tom Poker – the bogey man, the terror of naughty children who inhabits dark cupboards, roof spaces, under-stairs spaces (commonly called *poker holes*)

Tom-tit – the wren or titmouse

Toothsome – palatable, tasty

Totty, totty-headed – dizzy, particularly
after too much drink

Trape – to trail or be dragged along

Trattles – small pellets of dung, from sheep,
rabbits, hares etc.

Trickle or truckle – to roll or wheel. Hence *truckle-bed* –
a small low bed on wheels that is kept under the main bed
and rolled out at need

Tricky – mischievous, spiteful

Trig – to trot gently, as a small child might after
its mother

Tutter – trouble, fuss

Twiddle – to be busy with trifles

What are you twiddling about with there?

Twilt – a quilt

Twit – a snappish fit of ill-humour

Tye – a large area of common pasture, once frequently
found in central Suffolk and still found in place names

U

Undeniable – unexceptionable; something with which no
fault can be found

Under-butter – the butter made with the second
skimmings of milk. It doesn't keep well and is never sold
on, being kept for home consumption

Under-grub – to undermine

Uneathily – unwieldy, hard to propel into motion. May be applied to corpulent people

Unfaceable – unreasonable or indefensible. May be applied to proposals or arguments in debate

Ungain – intractable or inconvenient

Unsensed – stunned, as by a blow or a fall

Up-land – higher drier ground to the west of the county, as distinct from the lower and wetter fenland or coastal areas

Urgeful – urgent, important

Southwold floods, January 1905

V

Valour – value or amount, or esteem

Vast – a very great quantity

Verment – vermin

Viper's dance – St Vitus' dance

Voke – to retch or try to vomit

W

Wage – to urge or attempt to prevail on someone, especially to do something difficult or unpleasant

I would not do it, if you were to wage me to it.

Walk – an unenclosed field (from the ancient rights of sheep to walk over such land)

Wallop – to move as fast as possible, with great effort

Walter or wolter – to lie twisted and flat on the ground, as corn or grass after a storm

Wappet – a yelping dog or cur

Waps or wapsy – a wasp

Wards – calluses or hard skin on the hands or feet, deriving from hard labour or lots of walking

Water-bewitched – weak tea, coffee, punch etc. which is so diluted with water that the flavour is nearly imperceptible

Water-ranny – the field mouse

Weariful – tiresome, trying one's patience

Weary – feeble or sickly; or troublesome, vexatious

Weather-head – a second rainbow sometimes seen alongside a particularly strong primary rainbow

Weather-laid or weatherbound – prevented from going on an intended journey by inclement weather

Weer – pale, ghastly and ghostly in appearance

Wem – a fretted or frayed place in a garment

Wherret – to pester, annoy or harass

White herring – a fresh herring, untreated by pickling or smoking

Whittery – pale and sickly

Widdles – very young ducks

Wind-egg – an addled egg, or one without a yolk

Winge – to shrivel, as of fruit that is kept too long

Wishly – earnestly, with longing

Without – unless

Wolf – a gnawing pain, particularly in the stomach

Wood-lands – the higher country to the west of the county of Suffolk, as distinct from the lower and less wooded eastern coastal districts

Wood-sprite – the woodpecker

Word – to dispute or argue

They worded over it a long while.

Wret – a wart

Wrong – crooked, misshapen. May be applied to persons or to boughs of trees

X, Y, Z

Yale – a small quantity
Yangle – to tether a horse by fastening a foreleg and a hindleg together
Yarm, yawm or yawl – to shriek or yell, particularly like an enraged cat
Yipper – brisk, jaunty

Pronunciation and usage

As with all dialects, native Suffolk speakers are rightly proud of their linguistic heritage. Indeed, there is an argument in favour of the fact that the Suffolk dialect is the oldest of all English dialects, since it is where the English (the Angles) first settled, and where the Angles and the Saxons first mingled their communities and languages to form the basis of the English that we all speak today. Suffolk dialect contains influences from all the invaders or invited settlers who have ever arrived on these shores, from the Romans and the Vikings, through the Angles and the Saxons to the Normans and the Dutch. However, the history of the area goes back much further, with evidence of extensive Neolithic settlement and industry to be found in the hundreds of mineshafts of Grimes Graves, once a thriving centre of the flint-mining industry.

There is sometimes a tendency for the East Anglian dialects (particularly Suffolk and Norfolk, but sometimes Lincolnshire and Cambridgeshire as well) to be lumped together into a single amorphous "rural-speak", often caricatured in the media and indistinguishable from similarly bastardised West Country dialects and accents. However, as anyone who has spent time in East Anglia will attest, the local dialects are distinct; they do survive, albeit in diluted form, and the local pride in them is as strong as ever. Indeed, there is still a tendency to refer to foreigners, those whose misfortune it was to be born and raised outside the Three Counties (Norfolk, Suffolk and Essex), as shere-men. Indeed, Suffolk natives used their ears to identify such unfortunates: *I knew he was a shere-man by his tongue*.

Bressingham village smithy, c.1900

The sing-song lilt and slow speed of the Suffolk dialect have led many to assume that its native speakers are likewise slow of wits. However, they could not be more wrong; Suffolkers are in fact possessed of a highly sophisticated sense of humour, often delivered in the form of deadpan one-liners at the expense of unwitting foreigners. In fact, the characteristic rise and fall of the Suffolk intonation, often including a rising inflection on the last syllable of a statement so that the speaker sounds as if they are asking a question, is one of the features which distinguishes the Suffolk dialect from that of its sister county Norfolk (which has a distinctive drawling intonation in comparison).

The dialect often involves dropping sounds within words – so that dew becomes *doo*, queue becomes *koo* and tune becomes *toon*. Initial syllables are sometimes lost and replaced with glottal stops and vowel sounds may be lengthened, so that tomorrow becomes *amara*. There is a distinct tendency for native speakers of the Suffolk dialect to jumble or cram words together, forming new portmanteau-type words in the process. In rural Suffolk in the eighteenth century a girl was once employed to keep cows, a task more commonly allotted to boys. She described herself as a *galcobar*, a word which puzzled local dialect scholars until it was discovered on further questioning that she meant she was a girl-cowboy. The dialect is also prone to double negatives. Suffolk folk who have given up bad habits may be heard to state that *I dunt do that no more*, while a farmer was once heard to complain in a bad year that *I have no apples to year, no pears, no plums, no cherries, no nuts, no nothing at all.*

The accepted past tense forms of verbs are rarely used in Suffolk, with the exception of to be and to have. Most verbs simply take the present tense form, but some have their own particular forms, so that *She say she shew me* means She said she showed me. Likewise, to ride, to freeze and to rise are further examples, with their usual past participles being replaced by *rid*, *friz* and *riz* respectively. Certain words came into usage because of their metaphorical meanings, but they were sometimes also understood literally. For example, a *wolf in the stomach* was the phrase used to describe someone who has excessive hunger or craving for food. However, the word wolf might also have been applied to describe a gnawing pain in the stomach, such as might be caused by a disease or ailment. One old Suffolk woman described in all seriousness that her husband had had a wolf in his stomach, but the doctor found it and carried it away. Far from the metaphorical image, the old woman apparently believed that an actual animal had somehow found its way into her husband's stomach but the doctor had been able to prevail on it to leave.

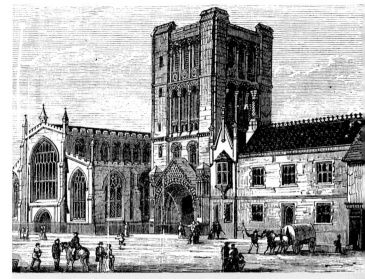

An engraving from 1890 showing one of the gates
into Bury St Edmunds.
Shutterstock ©Morphart Creation

There are a few examples of the Suffolk dialect set down
phonetically by its native speakers. One of the shortest and
pithiest was a sign above the door of a chandler's shop in
Drinkstone, near Bury St Edmunds, recorded by the local
newspaper in 1776:

Hear liss one woo cuers a goos.

Gud bare bako sol hare.

The translation was generally agreed to be: Here lives one
who cures agues. Good beer and tobacco sold here.

History, traditions and customs

Suffolk has a rich history of seagoing trade in goods such as wool, as well as a once-thriving fishing industry centred around ports such as Lowestoft (pronounced *Lewst'ff* by the locals) and Felixstowe, still a gateway to the continent with its ferry port. In fact, during the seventh and eighth centuries the kingdom of the East Angles was ruled from the international trading port of Dunwich, on the coast between Southwold and Aldeburgh.

Coastal erosion and violent storms have now reduced the once-busy settlement to a small village of only a few souls (one particularly vicious event in 1247 is known to have swept around four hundred houses into the sea, and at least nine chapels, churches and priories have been lost), but visitors still come to see the remaining ruins of the ancient town. Dunwich was not the only settlement lost to the sea, however; throughout eastern Suffolk there are records of houses, churches and roads being inundated and washed away during the high tides and heavy storms which plague this exposed stretch of coast.

THORPENESS HIGH TIDE 1911
MORTONS HOME 1911

A house lost to the sea, Thorpeness, 1911

Bess or *Tom o'Bedlam* were names given to wandering beggars, often wild and disorderly and named after Bethlem Royal Hospital, the well-known institution for the treatment of the mentally ill. These previous inmates of the hospital were not thought to be dangerous and had been given leave to roam freely during their more lucid moments, but they were supposed to return to the hospital periodically. Also known as *Cousin Betty* or *Cousin Tom*, they would sometimes enter households uninvited when only the women and children were present, loudly claiming kinship with the family and trying to claim a free meal until the menfolk came home and turned them out. When they turned up in a village or community they were often given considerable alms contributions to go away; Robert Forby, an East Anglian scholar and philologist, described them as *"annoyances to every body, objects of great terror to many, and, from the general wish to be rid of them as soon as possible, were likely to collect considerable contributions."*

There are many stories and folk tales connected with the Suffolk countryside. One is the legend of Black Shuck, the colossal demonic hound who haunts coastal and fenland paths throughout the sister counties of Norfolk and Suffolk and is said to bring bad luck and even death for those who encounter him. However, in comparison with other areas of the country there is a relative dearth of spirits of the countryside; it has been suggested that this might be due to the fanatical and excessive Puritanism which took hold across East Anglia during the sixteenth and seventeenth centuries, and an associated repudiation of superstition and the occult. Indeed, Matthew Hopkins, who held the post of Witchfinder General during the English Civil War, was born in Great Wenham in Suffolk, the child of a Puritan preacher, and he is said to have hanged sixty women in his home county in one year alone.

Another, slightly friendlier tale is the story of two 'green children' who were found near the village of Woolpit. The village itself is said to get its name from the tale that the last wolf in England perished here in the twelfth century after being trapped in a wolf pit, and indeed it was near the wolf pits that the two terrified children with green-tinged skin were found. No one could understand their speech, and they were eventually taken to a local manor house where they would eat nothing but raw beans for a long time. The boy soon died, but the girl lived and grew to adulthood, her skin eventually losing its green colouring. She learned to speak English, and recounted a tale whereby she and her brother came from a land where there is no sun, but there is light like our twilight all the time. They were following their flocks and found a cave, which they entered and heard the sound of bells. They were so entranced by the music that they explored deeper and deeper into the cave, eventually reaching the entrance to our world. There they were blinded by the bright sunlight and stood rooted to the spot in fear until they were found by the villagers.

Some towns in Suffolk have a reputation for the shrewdness of their inhabitants, sometimes at the expense of their fellow Suffolkers. Newmarket is one such; there is an old story of a simple countryman who liked a game of dice, but who fell in with a party of canny Newmarket rogues who meant to con him. After losing a few times to his newfound friends the countryman became suspicious and insisted on examining the games pieces. With great simplicity of character he exclaimed, *"Hye! Hye! Here's a dee with tew douces!"* Unfortunately the Newmarket gang had the presence of mind to blame him for their own dishonesty, and he was beaten for his discovery.

Other towns and villages also provide sayings that were known county-wide. Walberswick is a small Suffolk port town on the river Blyth, and a *Walberswick whisperer* was understood to be someone who whispered very loudly and audibly. The joke suggested that a Walberswick whisperer could be clearly heard in Southwold, another sea-port town a mile or so distant from Walberswick across the Blyth estuary. One curiosity of Southwold is that it has been said to be the place where swallows leave these shores during their annual southward migration in the late summer. Huge flocks of them have been known to perch on the roof of Southwold Church while the wind is off-sea, blowing east to west, and waiting until it changes direction to carry them easily across the sea to Holland and thence southwards to Africa.

The charming rowing boat ferry across River Blyth between
Southwold and Walberswick
Shutterstock ©AnglianArt

Walberswick Village - The kissing bridge 1921

The violent and athletic game of camp, somewhere between football, rugby, boxing and all-in wrestling, was once played right across East Anglia, and local derby matches between the sister counties of Norfolk and Suffolk were keenly fought affairs, often involving serious injuries and even deaths among the players. Lord Rochford of Easton in Suffolk was known as a particularly keen patron of the game, but most communities had a camping ground set aside. Certainly Hawstead had a camping pightle mentioned in deeds from 1466, and in Stowmarket there was a large piece of land known as the camping land. Indeed, farmers often encouraged games on their land, since the play was considered beneficial to the turf.

The field of play contained two goals 120 yards apart, with equal teams usually consisting of twelve combatants. As Forby described it, the umpire tossed the ball between the teams, and then *"the contest for the ball begins, and never ends without black eyes and bloody noses, broken heads or shins, and some serious mischief."* The games were known to be excessively physically demanding, and were often limited to half an hour in duration. The game was encouraged by the local nobility; *"certainly no kind of manly exercise can display to so much advantage the powers, proportions and attitudes of a fine muscular frame."*

Rural fairs were common, accompanied by the usual community games and competitions – races, tug-of-war, animal and produce shows and so on. One Suffolk speciality were the so-called *sneering matches*, where people would compete to out-do each other by pulling the ugliest faces – *sneering* was the local word for pulling a face without the intention to insult, and these grinning and gurning competitions provided high amusement for competitors and spectators alike.

Mildenhall West Row sports day, tug of war, 1906

Children, families and the church

There were many stories and superstitions associated with family life. Country maidens in search of their true love would use the following rhyme or spell:

A clover of two, if you put in your shoe,
The next man you meet in field or lane
Will be your husband, or one of the name.

To find out if her beau really loves her, a Suffolk girl might throw apple pips into a fire while saying his name. If the pip makes a noise when it bursts this may be taken as proof of true love, but if it burns without a sound he has no real affection towards her. When the maid has caught her young man and they are planning their wedding, they must take care not to wed on Christmas Day if two other couples are already going through the ceremony on the same day. Suffolk lore says that if three couples wed on December 25th, one of the six will die during the ensuing year.

When children come along, the couple must be sure to carry the infants up a flight of stairs as soon as they are born. If this doesn't happen the child will never rise to riches; there are stories of nurses or newly-delivered mothers being so keen to complete this ritual that if there were no stairs available they would take the newborn in their arms and climb on tables or chairs instead.

Earl Soham village street, 1908

Like children everywhere, Suffolk youngsters had a variety of nursery rhymes and nonsense songs to accompany their games. The song to the ladybird or barnabee (as this common insect is known throughout East Anglia) has an extra few lines in Suffolk:

Ladybird! Ladybird! Fly away home!
Thy house is a-fire, thy children will roam!
List! List to their cry and bewailing,
The pitiless spider is weaving their doom!
Then ladybird! Ladybird! Fly away home!

One song, perhaps sung by an untalented singer but once said to be common in Suffolk, was the following, rather abrupt little number:

There was an old crow
Sat upon a clod:
There's an end of my song,
That's odd!

Being raised among god-fearing folk, children may have been reminded of the seriousness of the Sabbath with the following rhyme:

Yeow mussent sing a' Sunday,
Becaze it is a sin,
But yeow may sing a' Monday
Till Sunday comes agin.

Rather than being threatened with the bogey man, children growing up in Suffolk may have been taught to fear the *clim*. This creature was a small mischievous imp that made its home particularly in the chimneys of nurseries or children's bedrooms, conveniently close at hand to be summoned down the flue for the purposes of scaring unruly children into good behaviour. Other areas of the home, usually dark enclosed spaces, were known as *poker holes* and were inhabited by the terrifying *Tom Poker*, who would lie in wait for naughty children and who might even be invoked by exasperated parents.

Children in farming families were usually given jobs on the land at an early age, and one of those given to the youngest boys was bird-scaring or crow-keeping. Sometimes the boys would have wooden rattles (in which case they were known as *clapper-boys*) or old shotguns loaded with powder and small pebbles, but often they would rely on their own voices, patrolling the fields and *"lustily whooping"* to scare the crows away from the newly-sown land.

There were many peculiarly Suffolk delicacies made to grace the tables of Suffolk farmhouses, mostly products of the county's rural heritage. Bacon and gammon made with black treacle, known locally as *black'uns* and still produced according to traditional methods in one or two places, were a well-known local treat. *Apple-jack* or *apple-john* were two names for the same dessert – a baked apple encased in pastry. However, strictly speaking *Suffolk bang* (or *Suffolk thump*) may not have been classed as a delicacy. This was the name given by men serving in the Navy to the particularly hard cheese produced by Suffolk dairy farmers. It was said to be so hard and dry that it banged when it was knocked against a table – or, alternatively, so hard that even the weevils couldn't eat it. An old rhyme describes it eloquently:

> *Those that made me were uncivil,*
> *For they made me harder than the devil.*
> *Knives won't cut me; fire won't sweat me;*
> *Dogs bark at me, but can't eat me.*

The texture of the cheese was thought to be so hard because it was made with milk that had previously been used to make butter – which, happily, enjoyed a very good reputation. The Suffolk dairy farmers were a canny bunch, though – they sold the inferior bang off to the Navy, and kept the better quality *spending cheese* for their own family consumption.

Many households observed particular customs related to the time of year, especially in relation to the type of food that was prepared or eaten. On Christmas Day in High

Suffolk (the higher lands to the west of the county, away from the coast) the housewife's first duty was to prepare a pot of *frumenty*, an ancient dish made from boiled cracked wheat enriched with milk, eggs, sugar, spices or orange. Hot elderberry wine would be served to visiting friends over the holiday season, while Whit Sunday would be celebrated with baked custards or gooseberry pies.

There are many churches in Suffolk, both in villages and in towns, where the celebrations of the year would be marked by families and communities. However, the clergymen of the county were not always distinguished by their sobriety and good behaviour. Bishop Blomfield, who grew up in Bury St Edmunds and held the living of Tuddenham in the early nineteenth century before becoming a Privy Counsellor and eventually Bishop of London, complained that drunkenness was a common charge against the Suffolk clergy. One individual was so drunk while conducting a funeral that he fell into the grave, while another had to be rescued by the Bishop's own servants when he became so intoxicated while visiting parishioners that he could not get himself home. A third, when he was rebuked for his drunkenness, replied, *"But my Lord, I was never drunk on duty!"* *"On duty?"* exclaimed the Bishop. *"When is a clergyman not on duty?"*

"True," replied the repentant man. *"I had not thought of that."*

Abbey Gate, Bury St Edmunds
Shutterstock ©Len Green

Blundeston Village Church 1917

Industry and agriculture

Suffolk has a proud seafaring history, encompassing not only fishing and trade but also ship-building; time was when the shipwrights of Ipswich and Woodbridge built domestic and industrial vessels and even warships, although the industry is long gone these days. The county also has royal connections, with Framlingham Castle and Kenninghall being favourite residences of Princess Mary before she became Queen Mary I.

Lowestoft, England's easternmost port and the easternmost point in the British Isles, has a long municipal rivalry with Great Yarmouth a few miles to the north, quarrelling over the herring fishery and heaping criticisms on each other based on the merits of their respective visitors. The Lowestoft fish markets saw a bustling trade, with trawlers and luggers from every part of the North Sea converging to unload their wares. East coast men mingled with Belgians, Dutchmen, Frenchmen and Scotsmen, with herring and mackerel packed into barrels and stacked high on the wharfs and the whole scene raucous with the cries of the salesmen and auctioneers.

A fishing boat on the beach at Aldeburgh
Shutterstock ©Richard Bowden

As well as fishing and legal trade the town has another underground history, with quantities of brandy, silks and laces finding their way ashore under the cover of darkness and resting in cellars or under nets until the excisemen were looking the other way. One particularly audacious scheme involved a French vessel which was sighted off Lowestoft harbour. A boat was lowered from the ship and rowed ashore, and as it reached land, the assembled beachmen and excise officials observed that it contained a coffin. The French sailors told a sad tale – the coffin contained the body of an Englishman who had paid for passage aboard their vessel, but who had been taken ill and died aboard. With his last breath the fellow had begged Monsieur le Capitaine not to bury him at sea, but to return him to his native shore so that he might rest in English soil.

The French boatmen transferred their cargo to the Lowestoft officials and rowed back to their boat, which soon departed. A parson was summoned and the beachmen and excisemen formed a mournful procession, bearing the coffin to the churchyard where it was laid in a hastily-dug grave. Fine words were said, the honourable conduct of the French captain was roundly praised, and even a few tears were shed over the grave of the unknown patriot. The following morning, however, the grave was discovered to have been opened and apparently desecrated – although it is questionable whether the removal of a consignment of silks, brandy and lace from the continent really constitutes a desecration.

The Butt and Oyster Inn, Pin Mill

In Suffolk the word *farmer* was commonly used to refer not to the owner or occupier of a farm, but to his eldest son, who was usually reckoned to be the eventual inheritor and was in the process of learning the trade. The owner himself was known as the *master*. Thus, a conversation between two labourers might go like this: *"Did the master set you on that job?" "No, the master didn't, but the farmer did."*

It used to be a custom in old Suffolk farmhouses that any labourer or servant who could bring a branch of hawthorn (or May blossom) in full flower into the house on the first of May would be entitled to a full dish of cream for breakfast. However, the custom fell into disuse, partly from the masters' disinclination to provide the reward, but also because it is highly unusual for the hawthorn to be in full bloom as early as the beginning of May.

The farming year was divided into *seals*, or times associated with a certain type of activity or crop. Thus there would be *wheat-seal* (a time for sowing or harvesting wheat), *barley-seal*, *clipping-seal* (the time for shearing the sheep) and so on. However, the word *seal* could also be extended to apply to hours of the day or night; a poacher might be described as being *out at all seals of the night*, while an industrious, punctual and sober man *keeps good seals and meals*.

Harvest seal near Stowmarket, 1916

Practical jokes were often played on hapless victims, particularly at times when large gangs of folk worked together. One such time was harvest, when it was a standing joke to ask some poor unfortunate to *"run and borrow a goaf-flap"* from the farmhouse. The goaf-flap was a wooden paddle or beater used to level the ends of sheaves of corn or straw (or *goafs*), but such a thing was rarely used in Suffolk – the 'left-handed screwdriver' of the county. The unsuspecting labourer would realise he was the butt of the joke from his reception when he knocked at the farmhouse door, and would then have to run the gauntlet of all his laughing comrades when he returned shamefacedly to the field.

Another harvest custom was an auction of all the rabbits that had been caught and killed during the reaping of the fields. William Dutt witnessed such a sale in north-east Suffolk and recounts the spiel of the auctioneer, holding up the creatures one by one:

> *Now then, you chaps, how much for thissun? Billy ha' dinged one o' its eyes in, but it's better 'an if a stowt had got it. Twopence – threepence fur thissun. Thas a tidy bit cheaper'n snarin' em an' gitten fined ten bob for trapesin in sarch o' conies, ain't it, Tom? You oughter know. Hull us yar crome here, Billy, I want suffin to knock 'em down with. My arms are beginnin' ter ache good tidily,*

a-howdin' up rabbits what nobody ont buy. Three left now – Billy, bor, yow'd better lave 'em at th' shop as yow go tru th' village; maybe Withers can make suffin on 'em.

The weather in Suffolk suffers from the same chill wind as the rest of East Anglia, whistling straight across the North Sea from the frigid north. An *ague in the face* is a common consequence of standing in the fact of a bitter Suffolk north-easter, directly from Siberia. There are many popular sayings regarding the weather, most referencing farming or agricultural practices. The Suffolk version of the old 'red sky at night' rhyme goes like this:

Evening red and morning gray,
Are sure signs of a fair day.
Evening gray and morning red,
Send the poor shepherd home wet to his bed.

A *burr*, or a misty halo around the moon, was thought to be a signifier of rain – the greater the burr, the heavier the rain: *Far burr, near rain; near burr, far rain*. The geographical position of Suffolk, with the sea to the east and many miles of exposed coast and flat country inland, contributes to its weather patterns: *When it rains with the wind in the east, it rains for twenty-four hours at least*. Locals needed to keep their wits about them to be ready for any eventuality; one elderly fellow always kept an eye on the weather as he worked on the land, and allowed that *"A kinder thowt as how we shall hev some downfall afore night, and my owd woman wunt hear o' my goin' to work 'ithout a coverin'"* (a raincoat or overcoat).

Polstead village, 1907

Birds and animals in Suffolk often had their own names. Finches were known as *alps* or *olps*, while country folk were in possession of many rhymes and homilies by which it was possible to mark the passing of the year. One such records the habits of the cuckoo, which arrives in the UK from tropical Africa in late March or April and departs again in July or August:

In Aperil – a shake as bill,
In May – a pipe all day.
In June – a change as tune.
In July – awah a fly;
Else in August – awah a must.

The Suffolk Punch, originally known as the Suffolk Sorrel, is probably the oldest pure draught horse in the world. The name comes from the word *punch*, an old Suffolk term for stocky and short; the breed is characteristically chestnut (or chesnut, as it is always spelled by the breed registries) in colour with white markings on the chest and legs, and was developed in the early sixteenth century for farm work. Suffolk Punches are usually shorter than other English draught horse breeds, such as Clydesdales or Shires, but they are immensely powerful and are known as good *doers*, having a reputation as excellent workers who will haul heavy loads until they drop. They played a part pulling artillery in both world wars, and have also hauled commercial vans and buses.

However, numbers dropped dramatically with the increasing mechanisation of farming in the second half of the twentieth century, and despite a recent resurgence of interest the breed is still listed as critically endangered by the Rare Breeds Survival Trust.

A Suffolk Punch stallion trotting in the field
Shutterstock ©Nicole Ciscato

Like the flint cottages in Norfolk, the sister county to the north, there is a particular style of Suffolk architecture. Suffolk white bricks were made from unique deposits of clay with a high quantity of chalk, which turns a creamy white when fired. They were used to create the facings of many fashionable and prestigious buildings during the eighteenth century and beyond; indeed, there are rumours that white bricks from Suffolk were used in the building of two rather famous white buildings in the US. Back in Suffolk, however, many buildings were painted Suffolk pink, a salmon-coloured paint traditionally made by adding red ochre and pigs' blood to the whitewash base.

Chelsworth Village 1909

Bibliography

Many writers have celebrated and preserved the Suffolk dialect, and as a consequence there is a wide variety of resources available. There is a broad range of modern material, written by enthusiastic and knowledgeable folk, but I have tried to go as far back as possible to track down antiquarian sources who experienced and recorded the ancient dialect as it was spoken tens or even hundreds of years ago, or to attested literary works which record the local vernacular in the dialogue of the characters. Among the most useful resources have been the following:

DUTT, WILLIAM: *Highways and Byways in East Anglia.* London: Macmillan, 1901.

FORBY, ROBERT: *The Vocabulary of East Anglia.* London, 1830.

GLYDE, JOHN JR.: *The New Suffolk Garland.* Printed for the author, Ipswich, 1866.

HALLIWELL, JAMES ORCHARD: *The Nursery Rhymes of England.* London: Warne, 1886.

HAYLOCK, CHARLIE: *Sloightly on th' Huh!* Newbury: Countryside Books, 2004.

MOOR, EDWARD: *Suffolk Words and Phrases.* London, 1823.

NALL, JOHN GREAVES: *Nall's Glossary of East Anglian Dialect*. Dereham: Larks Press, 2006.

YAXLEY, DAVID: *A Researcher's Glossary of Words Found in Historical Documents of East Anglia*. Dereham: Larks Press, 2003.

There is also a rich diversity of online resources, which have been collected and collated by many dedicated individuals. Among the most interesting are:

THE BBC VOICES PROJECT:
http://www.bbc.co.uk/voices

An interactive map with samples of recorded speech from different parts of Suffolk:
http://www.suffolkdialect.co.uk/maptest.html

Recordings of speakers from Suffolk (as well as other parts of the British Isles) made by the oral history pioneer George Ewart Evans between 1956 and 1977:
http://sounds.bl.uk/Oral-history/George-Ewart-Evans-collection

WICKHAMBROOK VILLAGE THATCHER AT WORK